TRAGEDY! TALES FROM THE TITANIC

Discovering Titanic

BY SARAH EASON
ILLUSTRATED BY KEVIN HOPGOOD

BEARPORT
PUBLISHING

Minneapolis, Minnesota

BEAR CLAW

Credits
20, © Wikimedia Commons/White Star Line; 21t, © Wikimedia Commons/Digiblue; 21b, © Wikimedia Commons/NOAA/IFE/URI; 22t, © Wikimedia Commons/Titanic Belfast; 22b, © Wikimedia Commons/Eva/Esther Hart; 23, © Wikimedia Commons/Taollan82.

Editor: Jennifer Sanderson
Proofreader: Katie Dicker
Designer: Paul Myerscough
Picture Researcher: Katie Dicker

Bearport Publishing Company Product Development Team
Publisher: Jen Jenson; Director of Product Development: Spencer Brinker; Managing Editor: Allison Juda; Editor: Cole Nelson; Associate Editor: Naomi Reich; Associate Editor: Tiana Tran; Art Director: Colin O'Dea; Designer: Kim Jones; Designer: Kayla Eggert; Product Development Specialist: Owen Hamlin

Statement on Usage of Generative Artificial Intelligence
Bearport Publishing remains committed to publishing high-quality nonfiction books. Therefore, we restrict the use of generative AI to ensure accuracy of all text and visual components pertaining to a book's subject. See BearportPublishing.com for details.

A Note on Graphic Narrative Nonfiction
This graphic story is a dramatization based on true events. It is intended to give the reader a sense of the narrative rather than a presentation of actual details as they occurred.

Library of Congress Cataloging-in-Publication Data

Names: Eason, Sarah, author. | Hopgood, Kevin, illustrator.
Title: Discovering Titanic / By Sarah Eason ; Illustrated by Kevin Hopgood.
Description: Bear claw books. | Minneapolis, Minnesota : Bearport Publishing Company, [2025] | Series: Tragedy! Tales from the Titanic | Includes bibliographical references and index.
Identifiers: LCCN 2024034184 (print) | LCCN 2024034185 (ebook) | ISBN 9798892328586 (library binding) | ISBN 9798892329484 (paperback) | ISBN 9798892328654 (ebook)
Subjects: LCSH: Titanic (Steamship)--Juvenile literature. | Titanic (Steamship)--Comic books, strips, etc. | Ocean liners--Great Britain--History--20th century--Juvenile literature. | Ocean liners--Great Britain--History--20th century--Comic books, strips, etc. | Shipwrecks--North Atlantic Ocean--History--20th century--Juvenile literature. | Shipwrecks--North Atlantic Ocean--History--20th century--Comic books, strips, etc. | Graphic novels.
Classification: LCC G530.T6 E27 2025 (print) | LCC G530.T6 (ebook) | DDC 910.9163/4--dc23/eng20240724
LC record available at https://lccn.loc.gov/2024034184
LC ebook record available at https://lccn.loc.gov/2024034185

Copyright © 2025 Bearport Publishing Company. All rights reserved. No part of this publication may be reproduced in whole or in part, stored in any retrieval system, or transmitted in any form or by any means, electronic, mechanical, photocopying, recording, or otherwise, without written permission from the publisher.

For more information, write to Bearport Publishing, 5357 Penn Avenue South, Minneapolis, MN 55419.

Contents

CHAPTER 1
A Watery Grave **4**

CHAPTER 2
Underwater Tech **8**

CHAPTER 3
***Titanic* Is Found!** **12**

CHAPTER 4
Up Close and Personal **16**

Finding a Ship of Dreams 20
More *Titanic* Stories 22
Glossary 23
Index 24
Read More 24
Learn More Online 24

CHAPTER 1

A Watery Grave

When it set sail for its first voyage on April 10, 1912, RMS *Titanic* was the biggest ship ever built. But just days into the journey, the wonder on water hit an iceberg and sank.

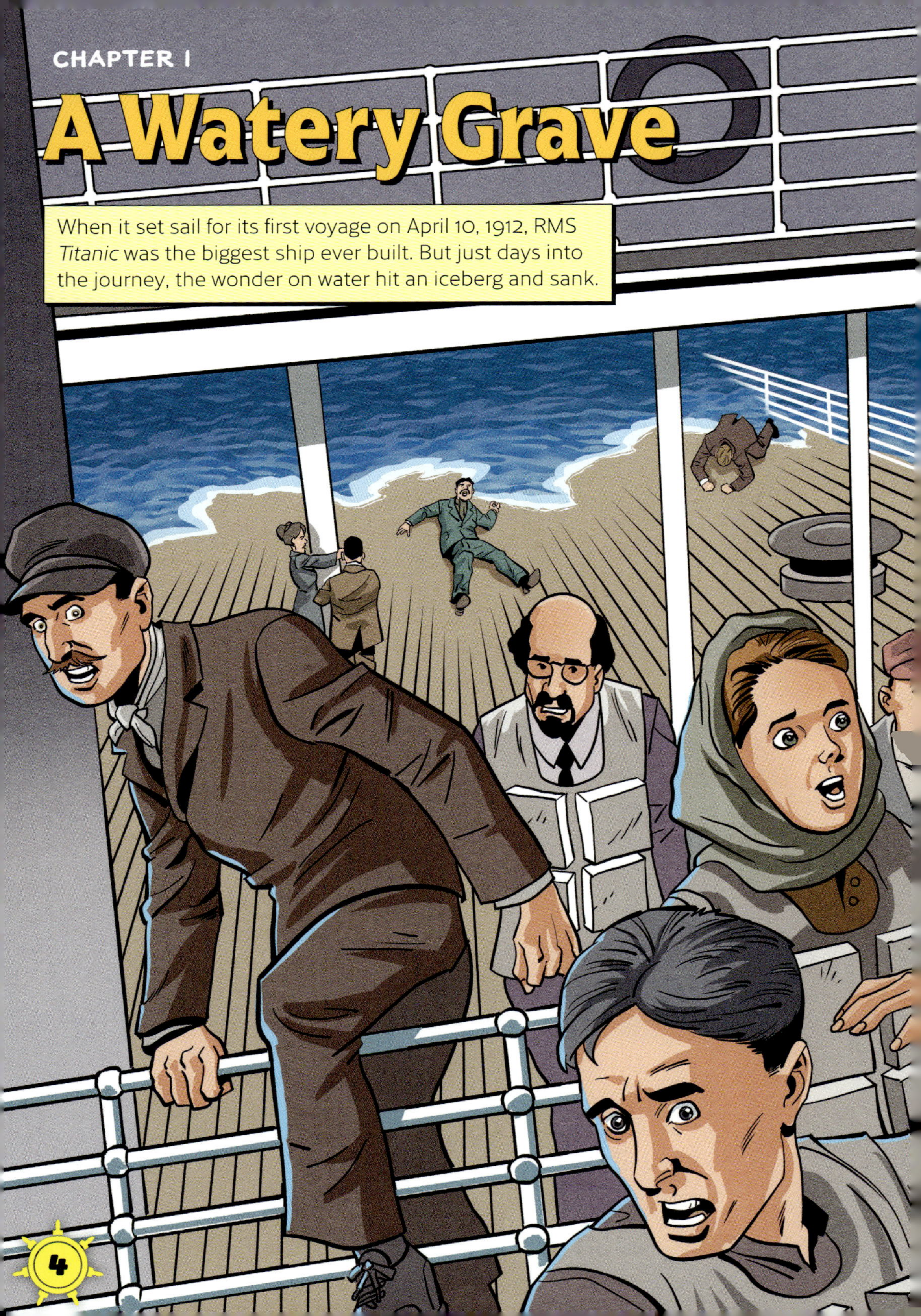

Out of the more than 2,200 people on board, at least 1,500 drowned in the freezing Atlantic waters. Many went under as the ship plunged below the waves.

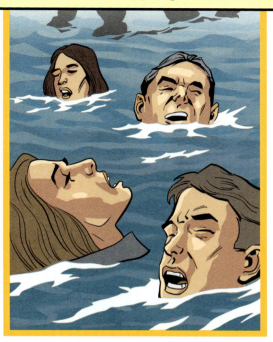

Around the world, people wondered if the **luxury** ship with its **elaborate** staterooms and detailed grand staircase would ever be seen again.

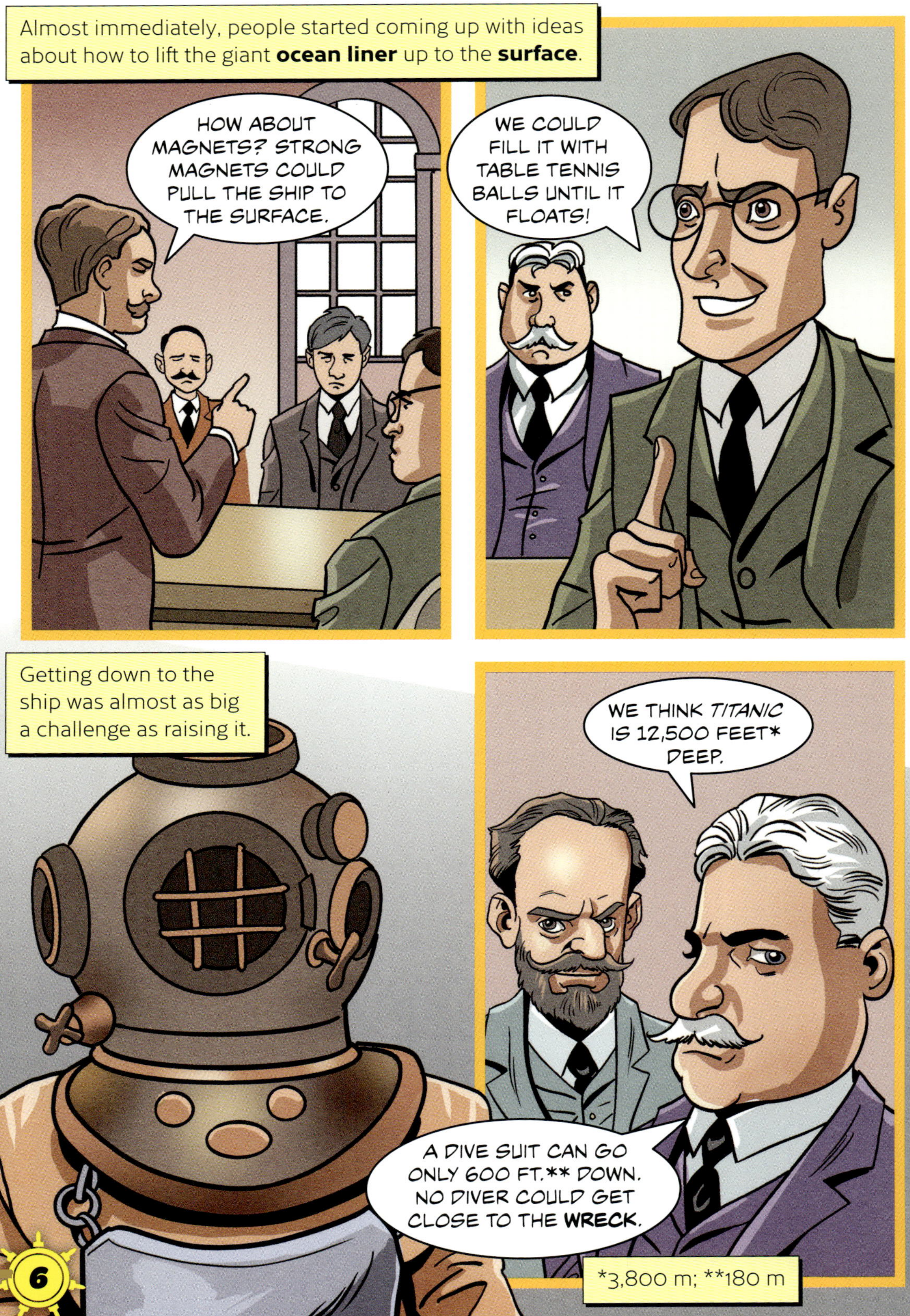
Almost immediately, people started coming up with ideas about how to lift the giant **ocean liner** up to the **surface**.
HOW ABOUT MAGNETS? STRONG MAGNETS COULD PULL THE SHIP TO THE SURFACE.
WE COULD FILL IT WITH TABLE TENNIS BALLS UNTIL IT FLOATS!
Getting down to the ship was almost as big a challenge as raising it.
WE THINK *TITANIC* IS 12,500 FEET* DEEP.
A DIVE SUIT CAN GO ONLY 600 FT.** DOWN. NO DIVER COULD GET CLOSE TO THE **WRECK**.
*3,800 m; **180 m

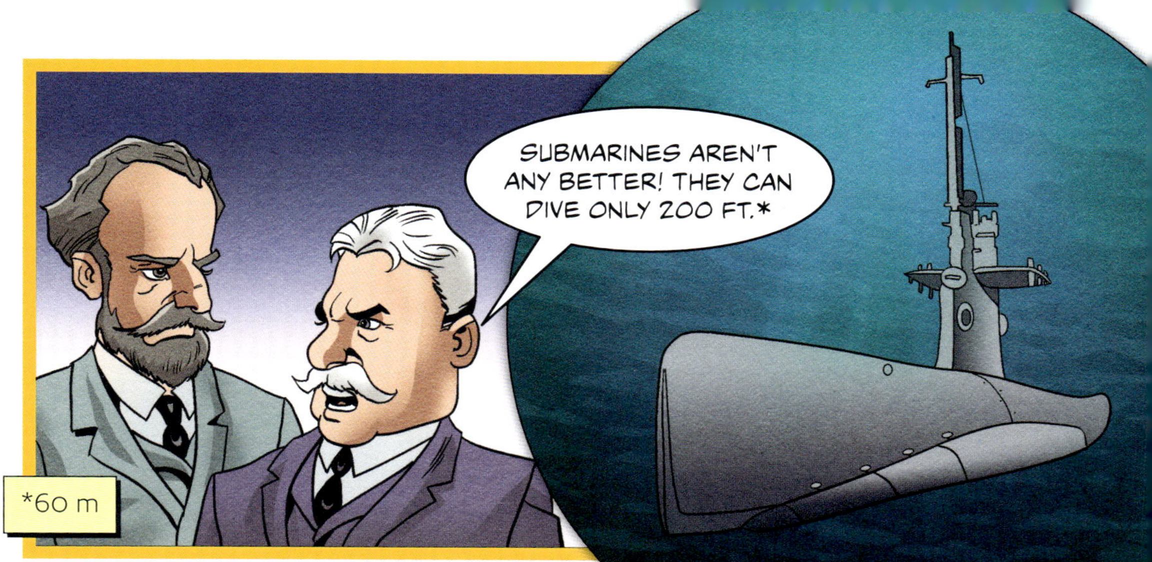
SUBMARINES AREN'T ANY BETTER! THEY CAN DIVE ONLY 200 FT.*
*60 m

But before any of that work began, scientists had to find where *Titanic* lay on the seabed. They knew the last location of the ship, but it was highly likely that the wreckage had drifted with the **currents**.

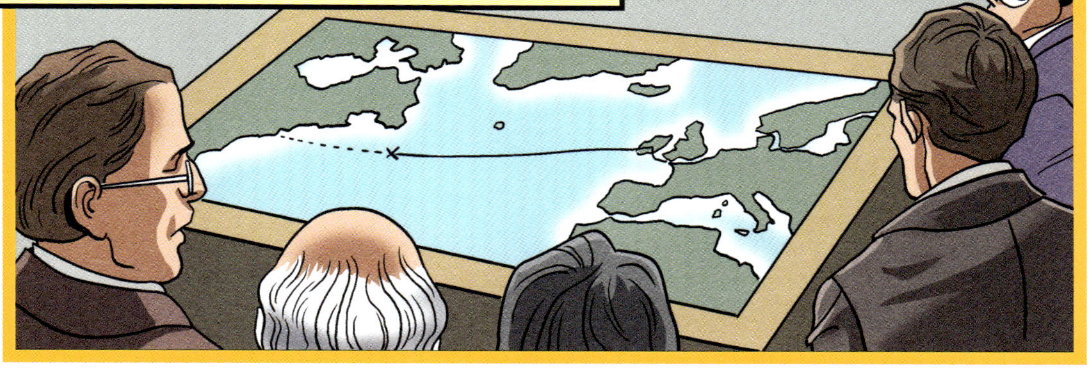

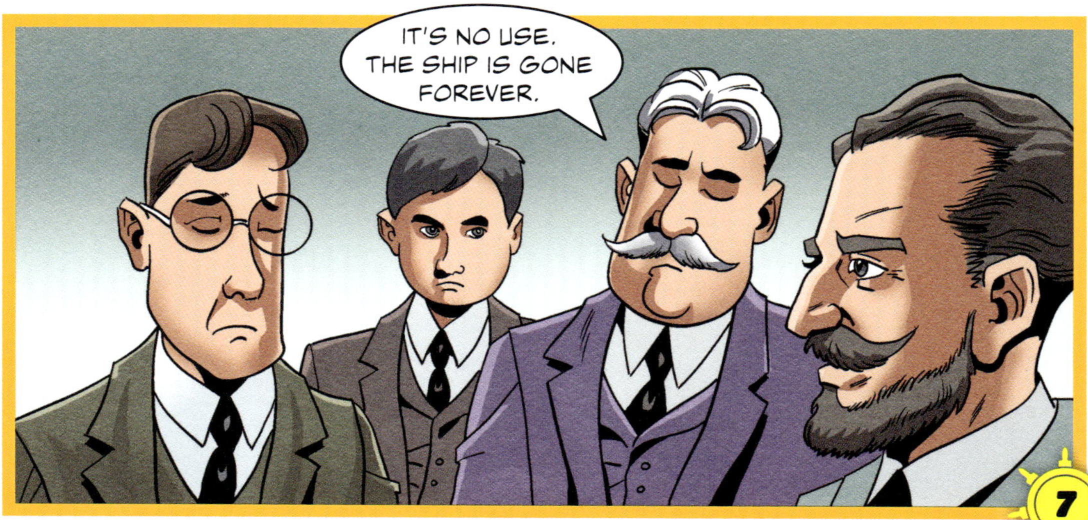
IT'S NO USE. THE SHIP IS GONE FOREVER.

CHAPTER 2

Underwater Tech

Then in the late 1970s, explorers had a new **innovation** that gave them hope—a video camera that could go deep underwater.

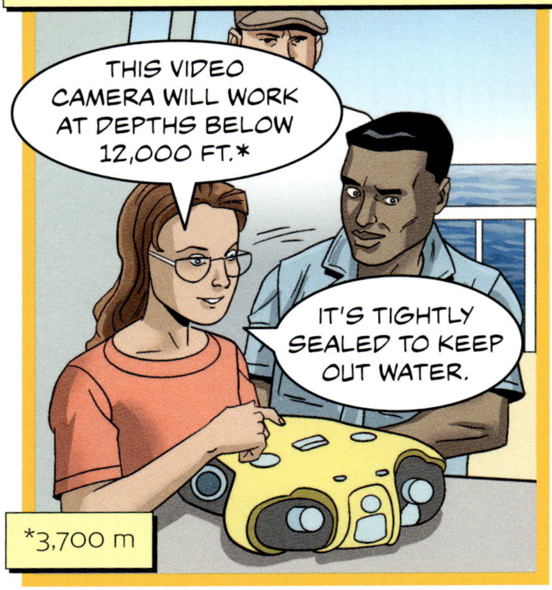
THIS VIDEO CAMERA WILL WORK AT DEPTHS BELOW 12,000 FT.*
IT'S TIGHTLY SEALED TO KEEP OUT WATER.
*3,700 m

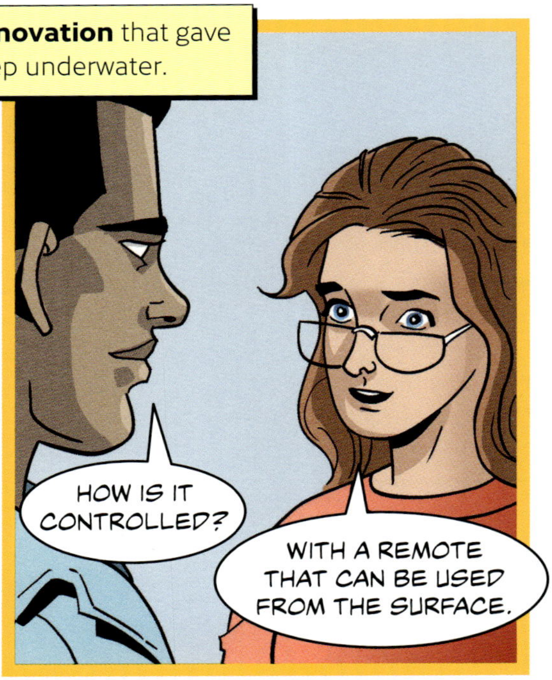
HOW IS IT CONTROLLED?
WITH A REMOTE THAT CAN BE USED FROM THE SURFACE.

And so, the search began. People started looking around where the *Carpathia* had picked up survivors in 1912.

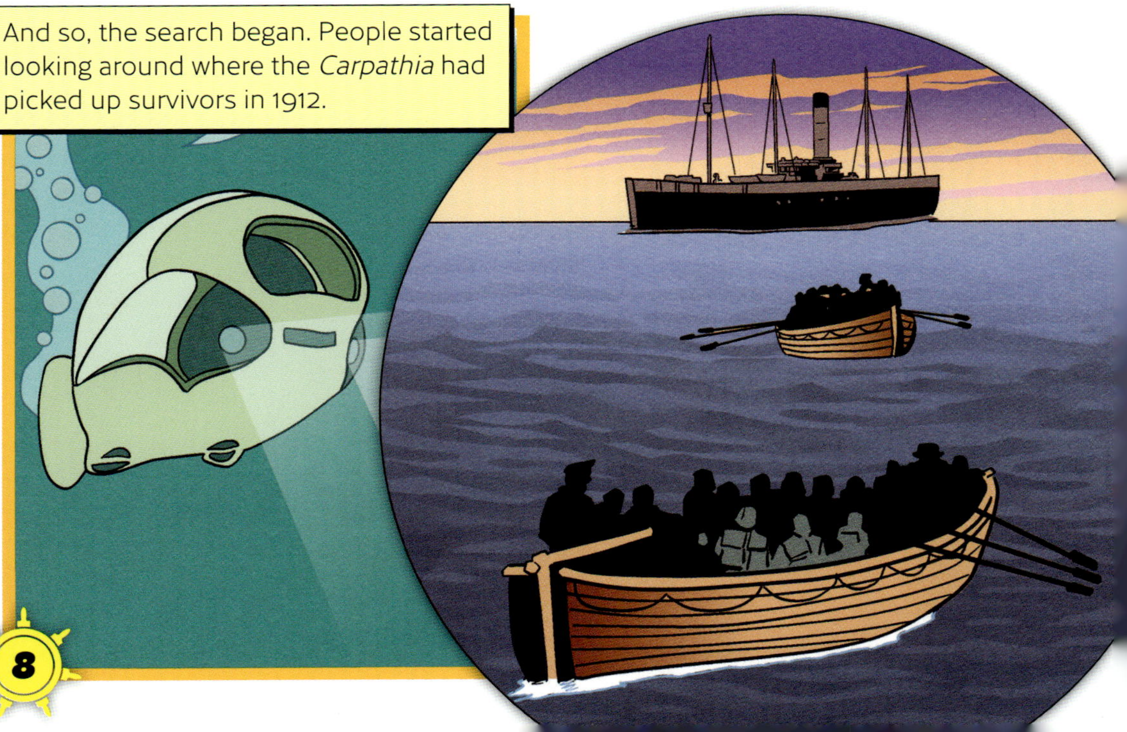

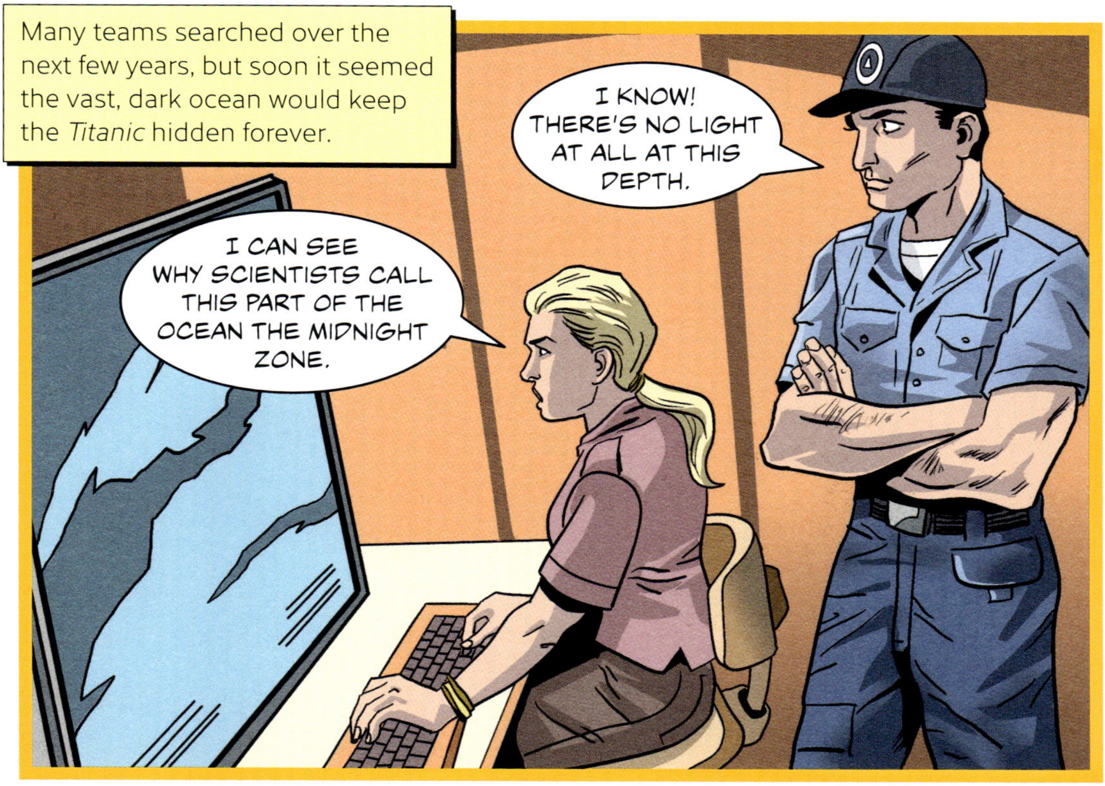
Many teams searched over the next few years, but soon it seemed the vast, dark ocean would keep the *Titanic* hidden forever.
I KNOW! THERE'S NO LIGHT AT ALL AT THIS DEPTH.
I CAN SEE WHY SCIENTISTS CALL THIS PART OF THE OCEAN THE MIDNIGHT ZONE.

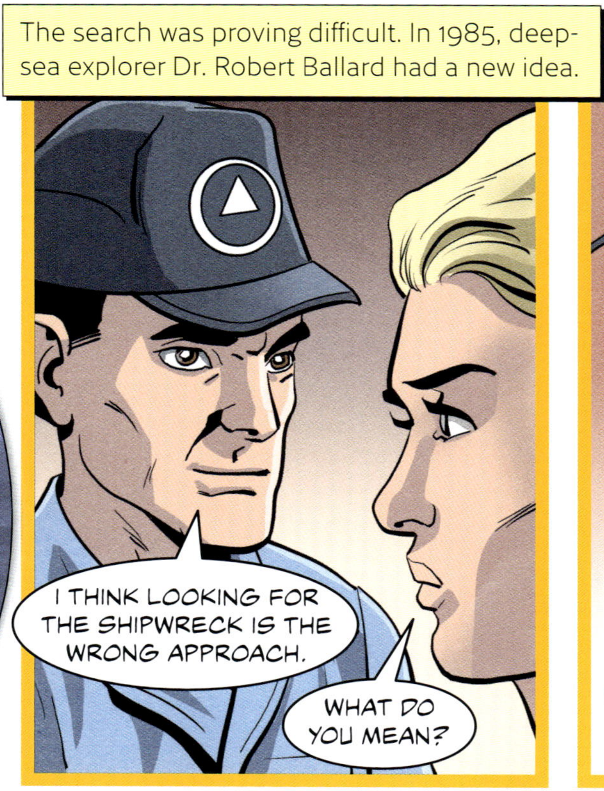
The search was proving difficult. In 1985, deep-sea explorer Dr. Robert Ballard had a new idea.
I THINK LOOKING FOR THE SHIPWRECK IS THE WRONG APPROACH.
WHAT DO YOU MEAN?

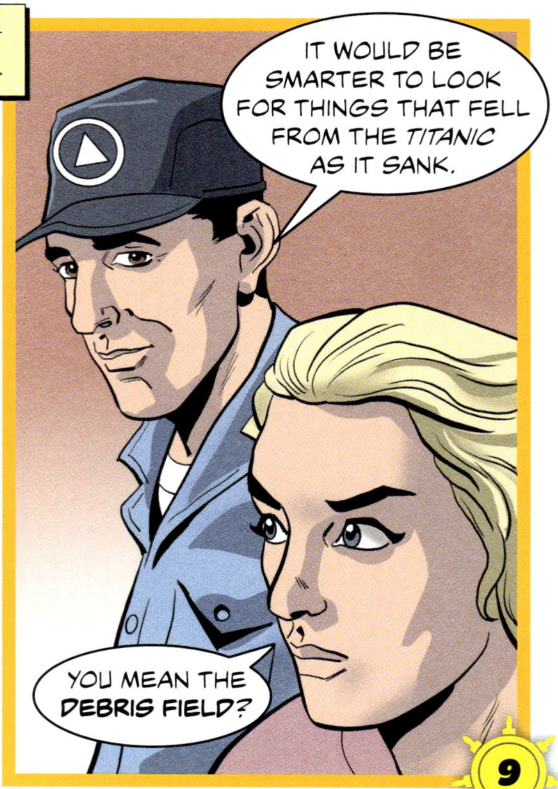
IT WOULD BE SMARTER TO LOOK FOR THINGS THAT FELL FROM THE *TITANIC* AS IT SANK.
YOU MEAN THE **DEBRIS FIELD**?

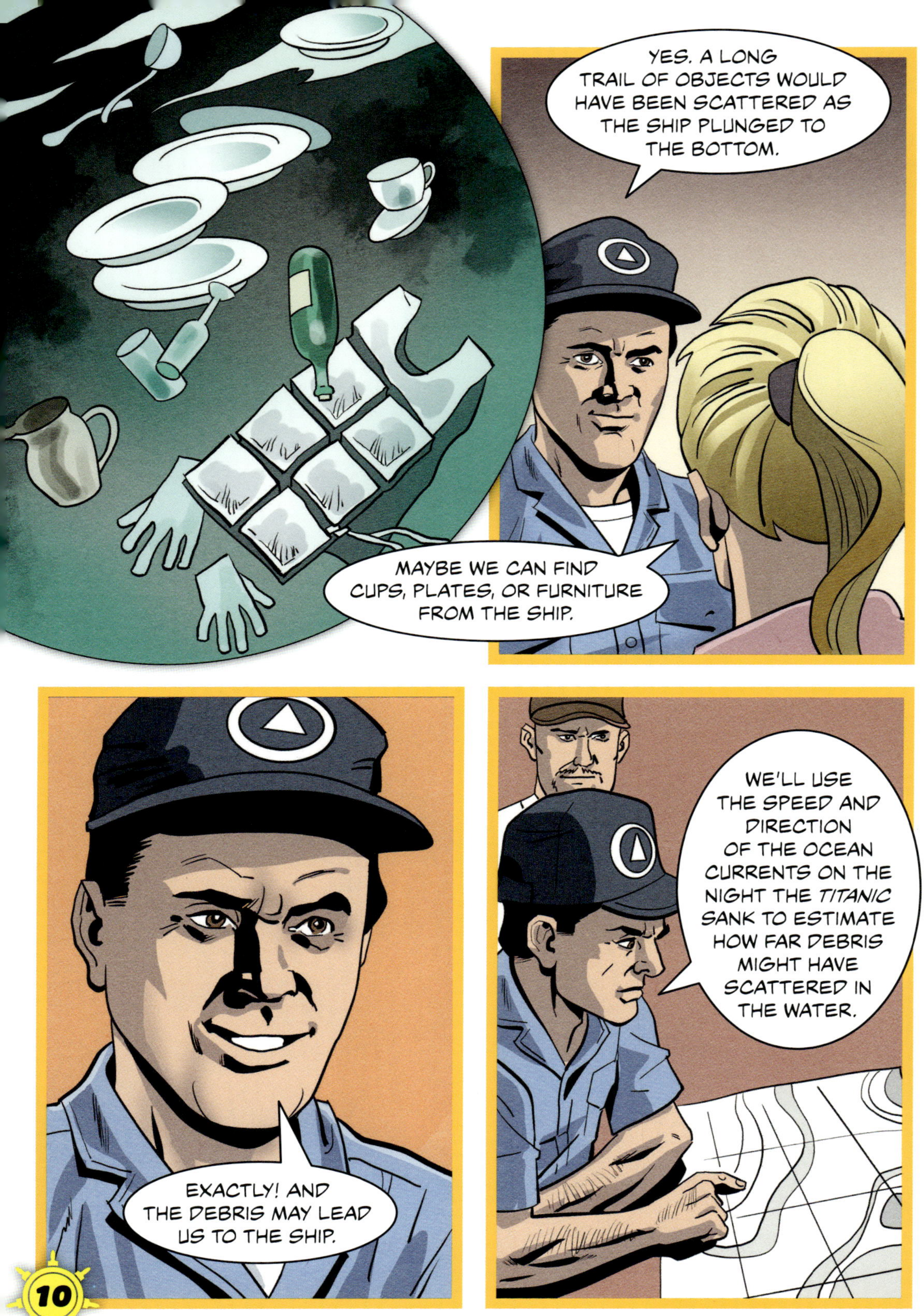
YES. A LONG TRAIL OF OBJECTS WOULD HAVE BEEN SCATTERED AS THE SHIP PLUNGED TO THE BOTTOM.
MAYBE WE CAN FIND CUPS, PLATES, OR FURNITURE FROM THE SHIP.
EXACTLY! AND THE DEBRIS MAY LEAD US TO THE SHIP.
WE'LL USE THE SPEED AND DIRECTION OF THE OCEAN CURRENTS ON THE NIGHT THE *TITANIC* SANK TO ESTIMATE HOW FAR DEBRIS MIGHT HAVE SCATTERED IN THE WATER.

On August 22, 1985, Ballard and his crew joined up with a French team of explorers led by Jean-Louis Michel aboard the U.S. Navy ship *Knorr*. Among the high-tech equipment was an uncrewed deep-sea submarine called *Argo*.

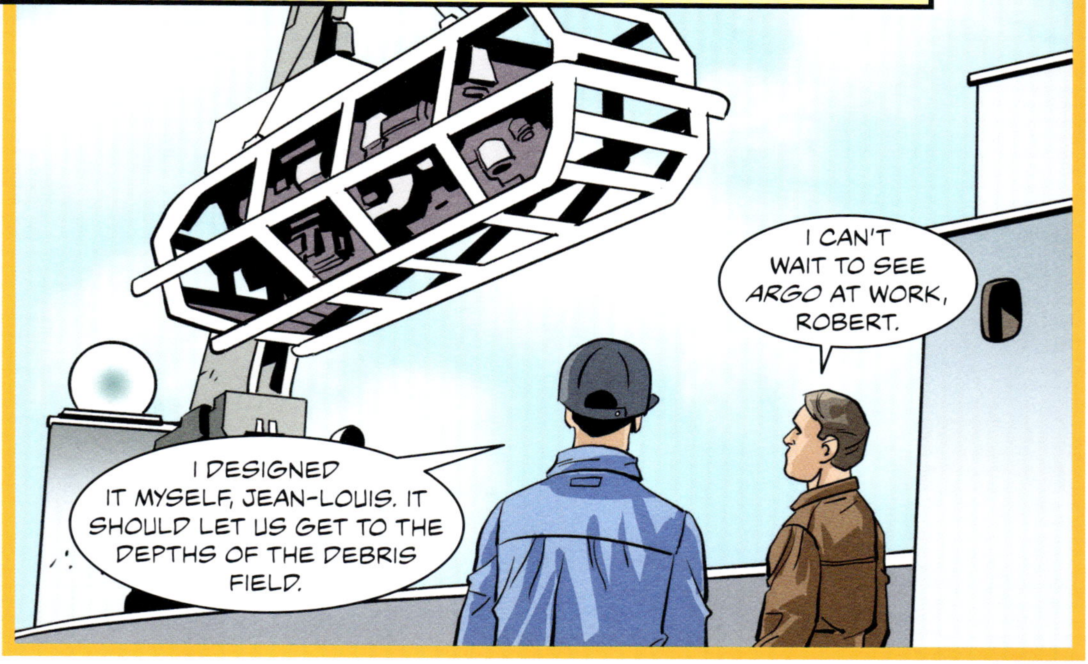
I CAN'T WAIT TO SEE *ARGO* AT WORK, ROBERT.
I DESIGNED IT MYSELF, JEAN-LOUIS. IT SHOULD LET US GET TO THE DEPTHS OF THE DEBRIS FIELD.

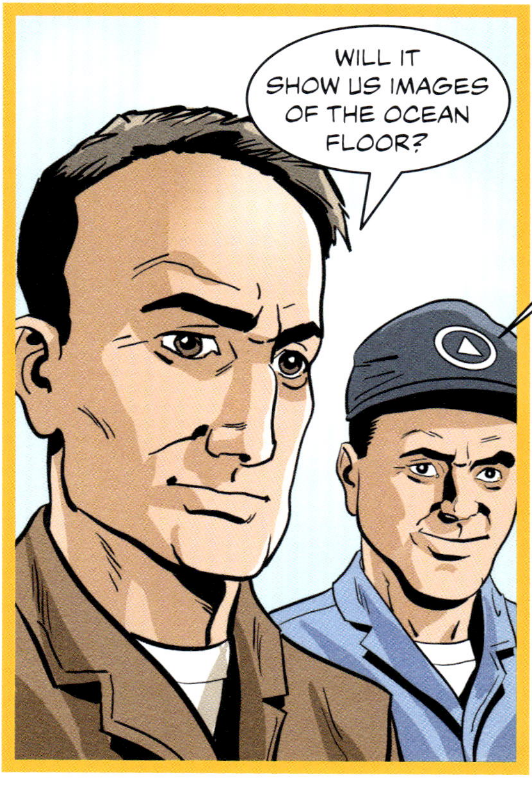
WILL IT SHOW US IMAGES OF THE OCEAN FLOOR?

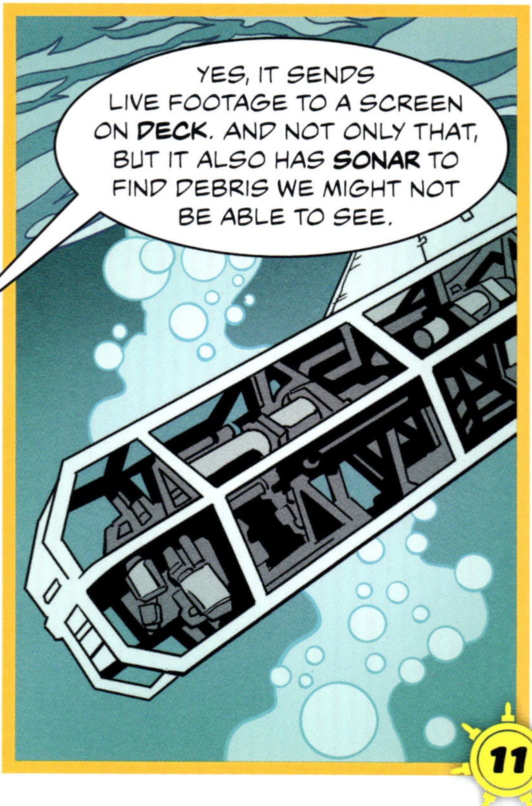
YES, IT SENDS LIVE FOOTAGE TO A SCREEN ON **DECK**. AND NOT ONLY THAT, BUT IT ALSO HAS **SONAR** TO FIND DEBRIS WE MIGHT NOT BE ABLE TO SEE.

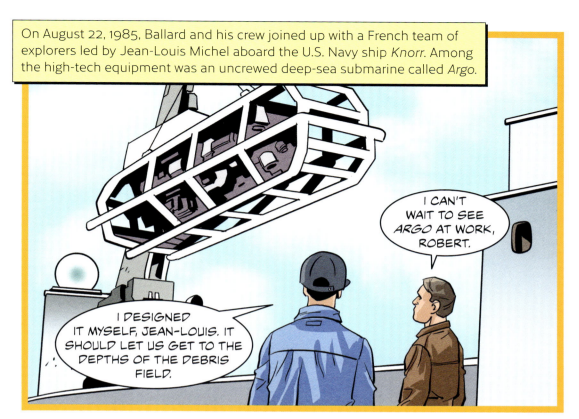

CHAPTER 3

Titanic Is Found!

Ballard and his team were excited. But after more than a week in the North Atlantic without finding anything, they were about to give up. Suddenly, early in the morning of September 1, something appeared on the video screen.

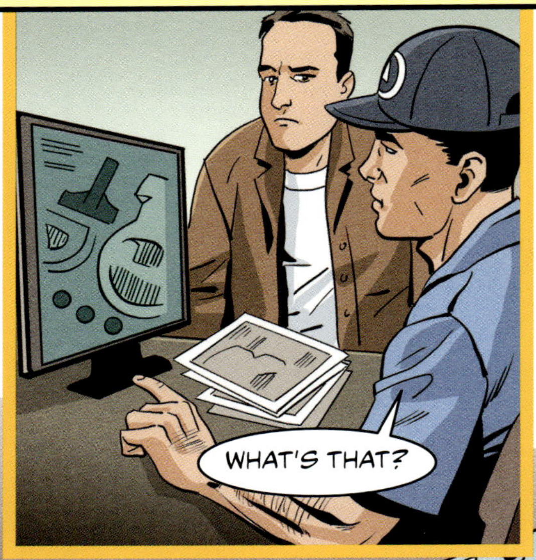
WHAT'S THAT?

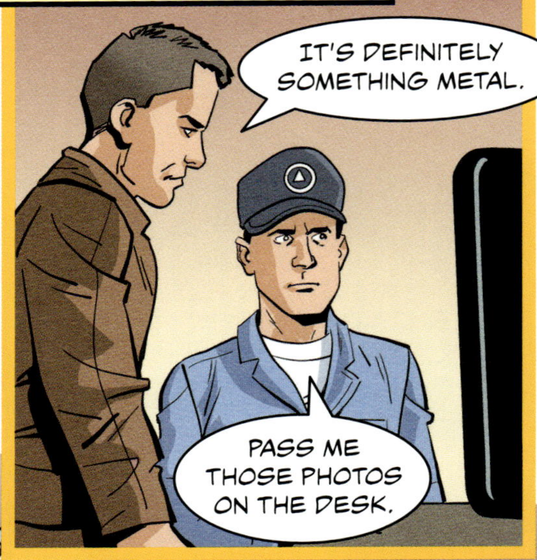
IT'S DEFINITELY SOMETHING METAL.
PASS ME THOSE PHOTOS ON THE DESK.

Ballard compared photographs of *Titanic*'s 29 boilers to what they were looking at on-screen.

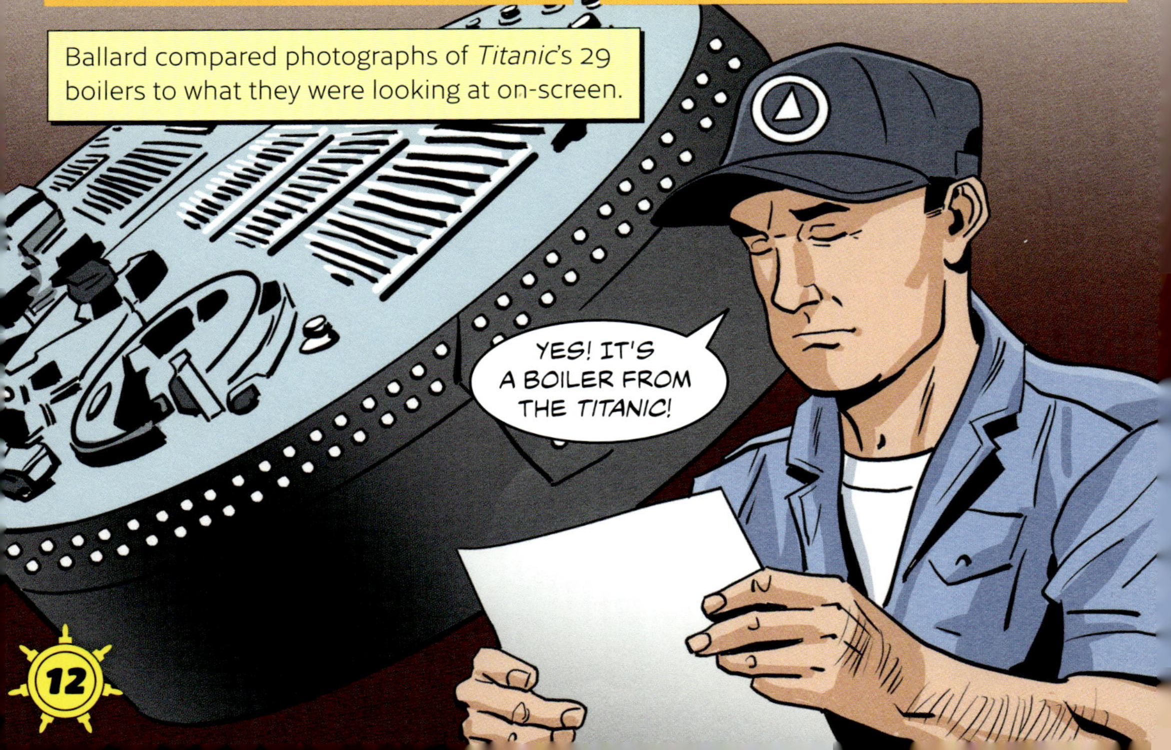
YES! IT'S A BOILER FROM THE *TITANIC*!

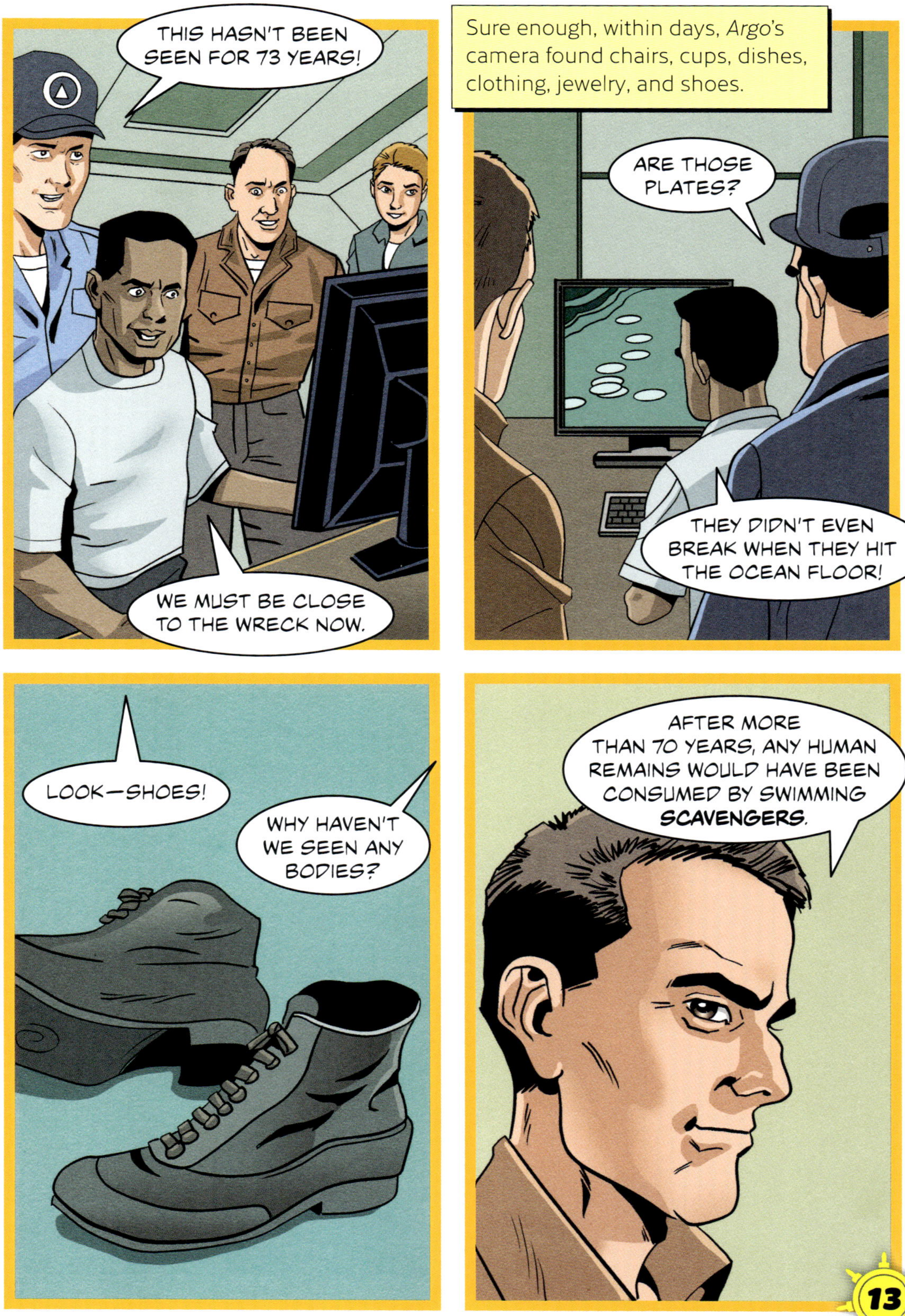
THIS HASN'T BEEN SEEN FOR 73 YEARS!
WE MUST BE CLOSE TO THE WRECK NOW.
Sure enough, within days, *Argo*'s camera found chairs, cups, dishes, clothing, jewelry, and shoes.
ARE THOSE PLATES?
THEY DIDN'T EVEN BREAK WHEN THEY HIT THE OCEAN FLOOR!
LOOK—SHOES!
WHY HAVEN'T WE SEEN ANY BODIES?
AFTER MORE THAN 70 YEARS, ANY HUMAN REMAINS WOULD HAVE BEEN CONSUMED BY SWIMMING **SCAVENGERS**.

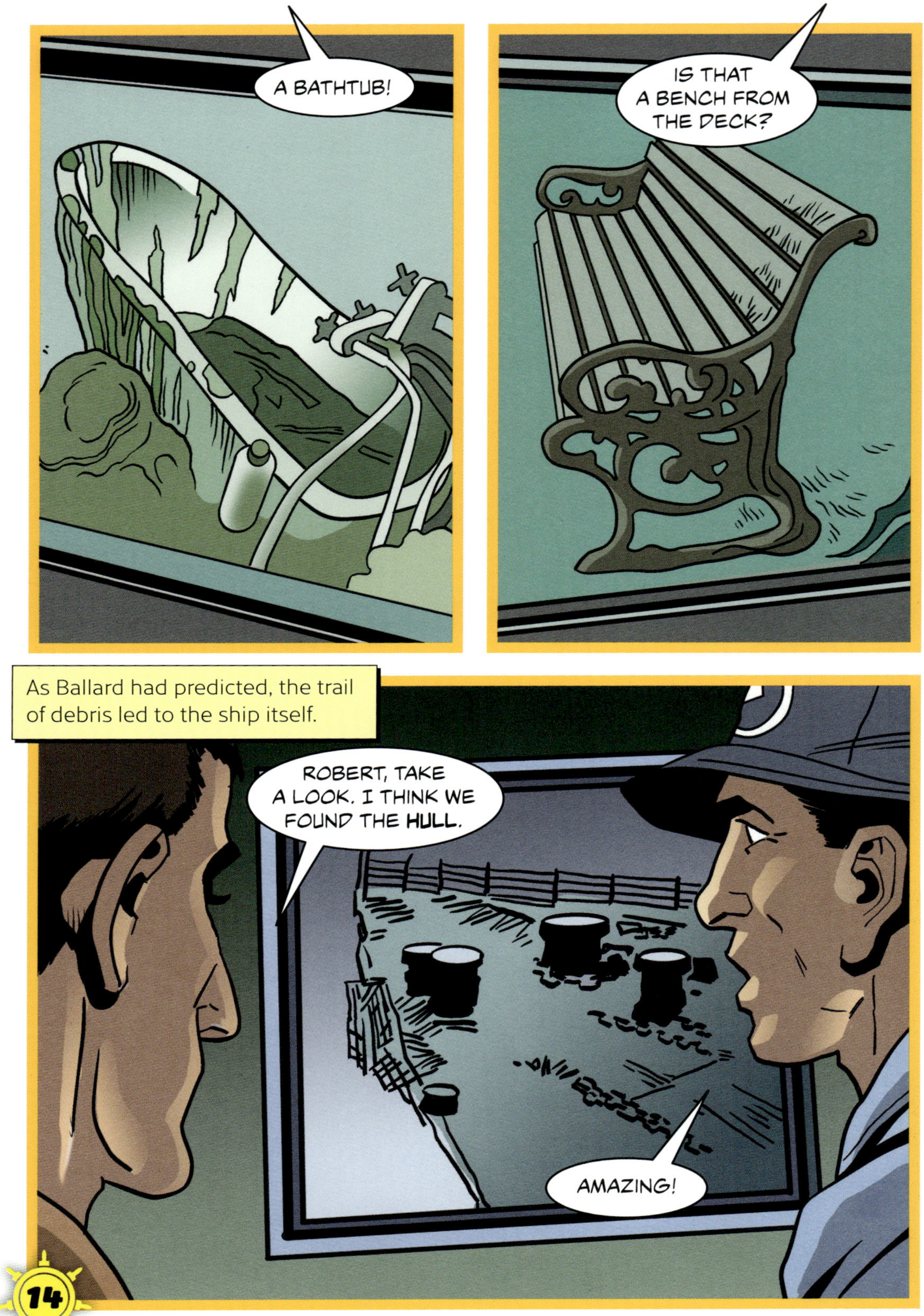
A BATHTUB!
IS THAT A BENCH FROM THE DECK?
As Ballard had predicted, the trail of debris led to the ship itself.
ROBERT, TAKE A LOOK. I THINK WE FOUND THE **HULL**.
AMAZING!

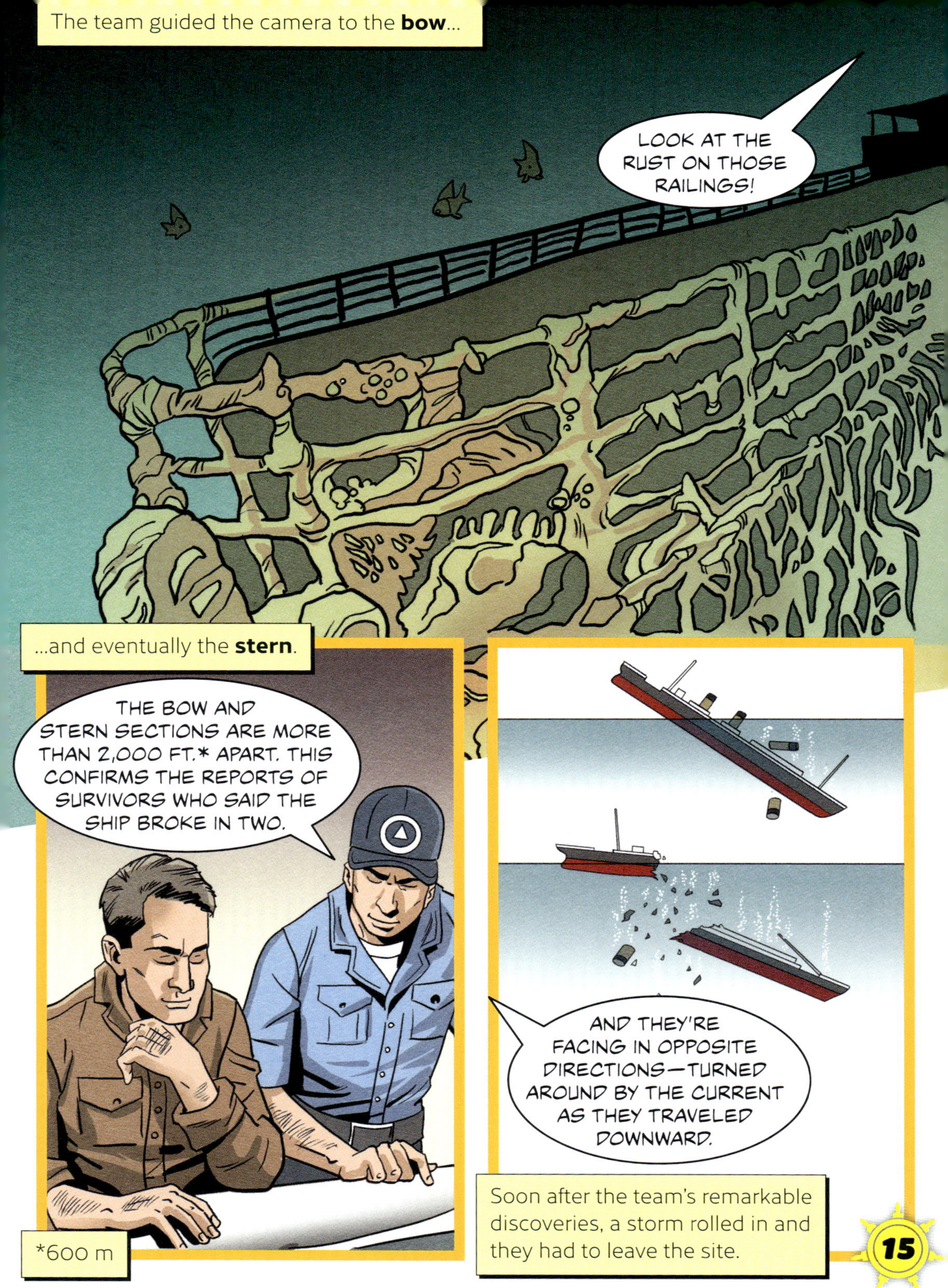

The team guided the camera to the **bow**...
LOOK AT THE RUST ON THOSE RAILINGS!
...and eventually the **stern**.
THE BOW AND STERN SECTIONS ARE MORE THAN 2,000 FT.* APART. THIS CONFIRMS THE REPORTS OF SURVIVORS WHO SAID THE SHIP BROKE IN TWO.
*600 m
AND THEY'RE FACING IN OPPOSITE DIRECTIONS—TURNED AROUND BY THE CURRENT AS THEY TRAVELED DOWNWARD.
Soon after the team's remarkable discoveries, a storm rolled in and they had to leave the site.

CHAPTER 4

Up Close and Personal

Ballard and his crew returned to the wreck of the *Titanic* less than a year later with *Alvin*, a deep-ocean **submersible** that could carry people.

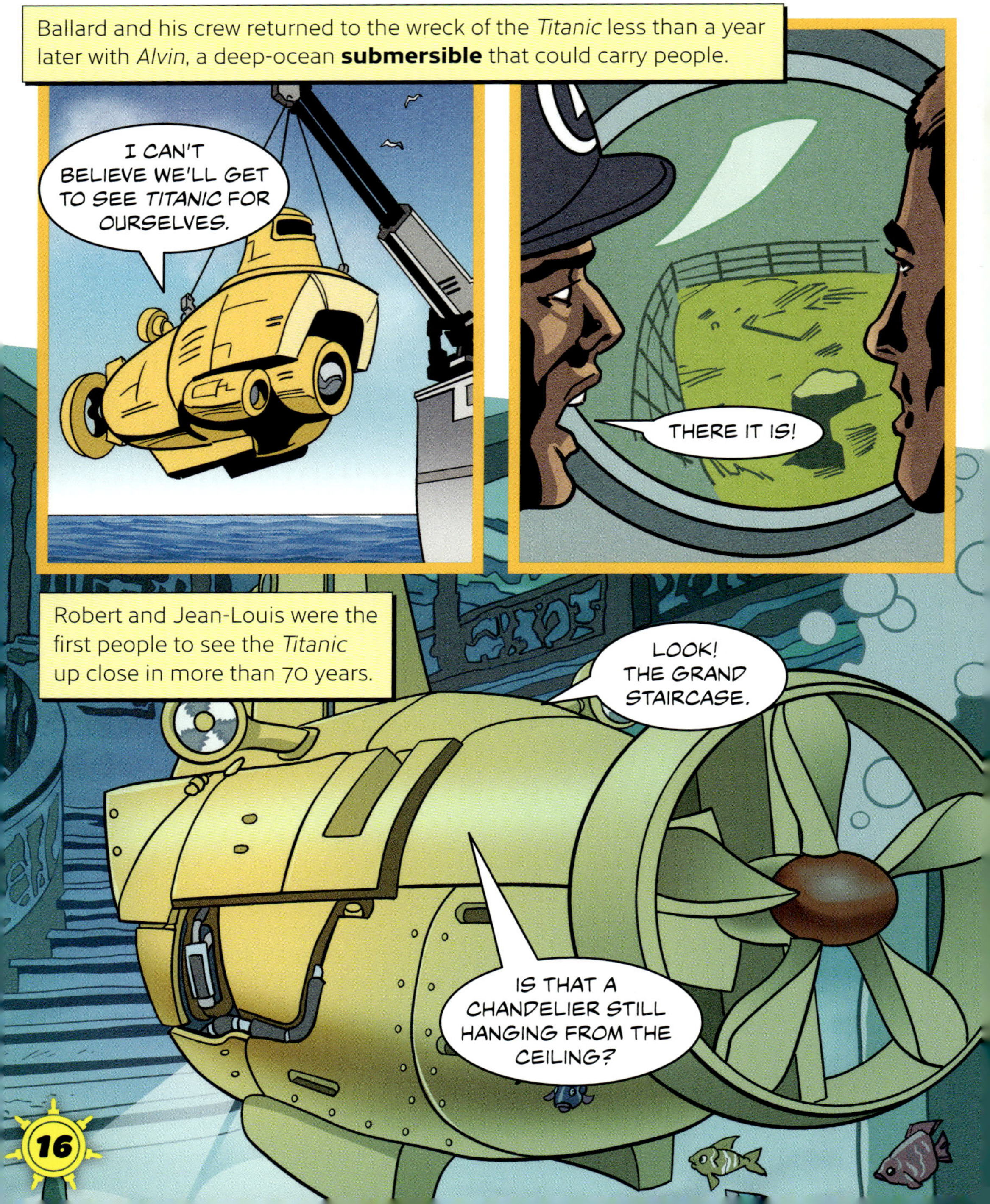
I CAN'T BELIEVE WE'LL GET TO SEE TITANIC FOR OURSELVES.
THERE IT IS!
Robert and Jean-Louis were the first people to see the Titanic up close in more than 70 years.
LOOK! THE GRAND STAIRCASE.
IS THAT A CHANDELIER STILL HANGING FROM THE CEILING?

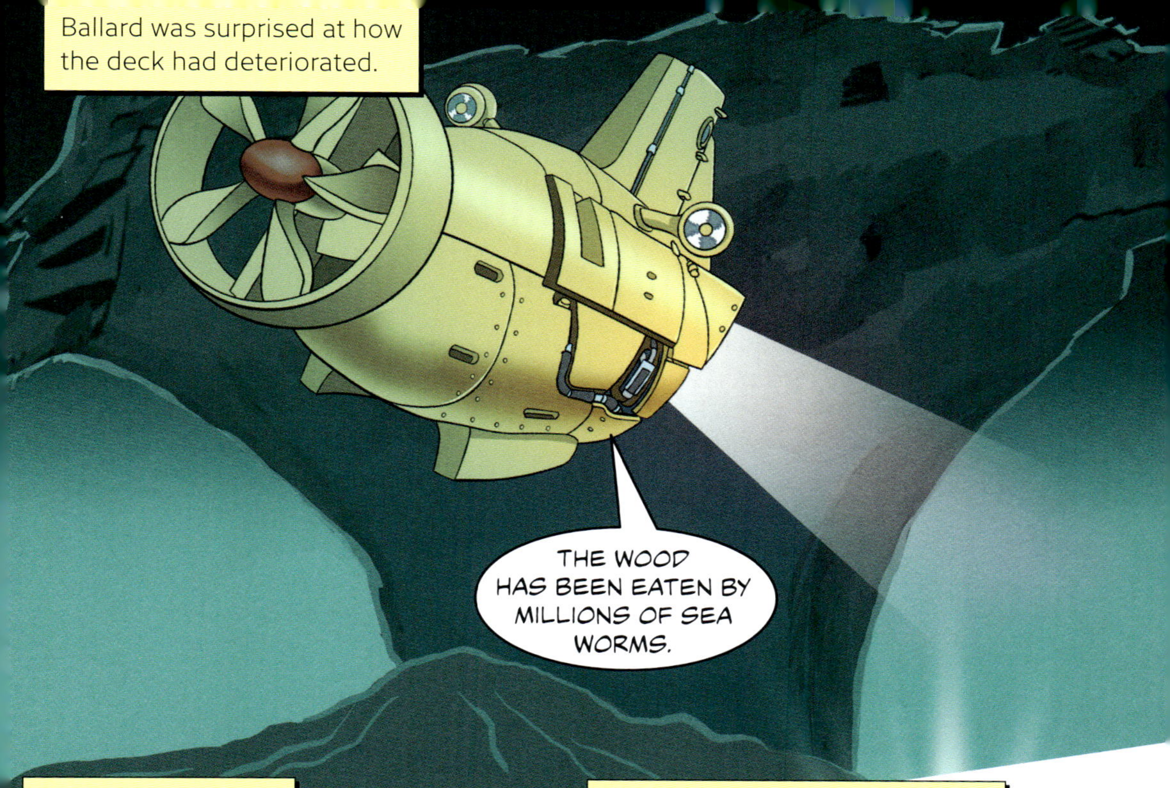
Ballard was surprised at how the deck had deteriorated.
THE WOOD HAS BEEN EATEN BY MILLIONS OF SEA WORMS.

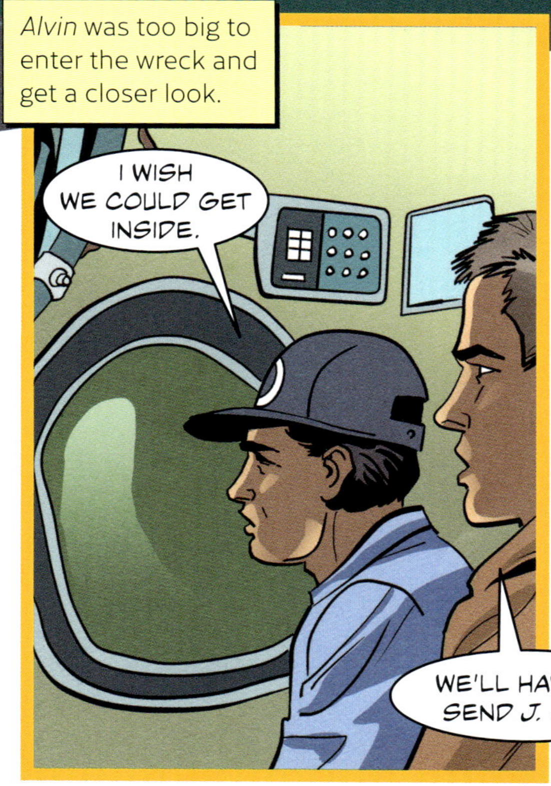
Alvin was too big to enter the wreck and get a closer look.
I WISH WE COULD GET INSIDE.
WE'LL HAVE TO SEND J. J. IN.

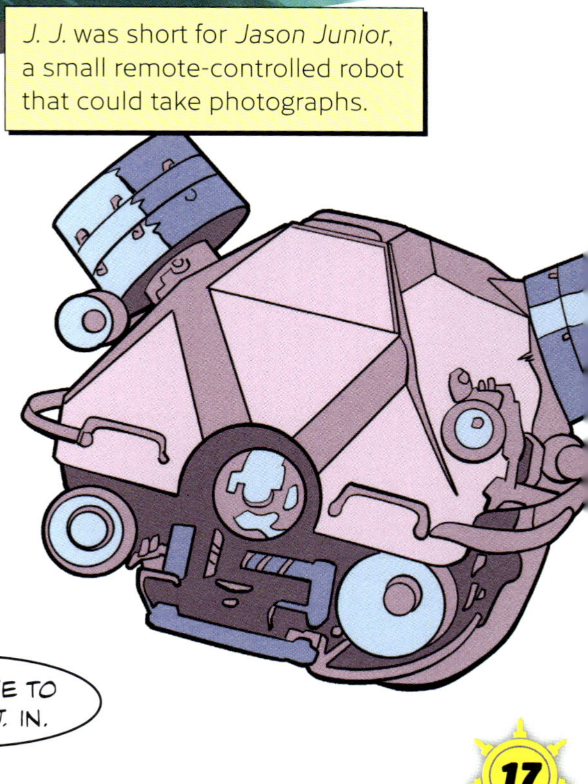
J. J. was short for *Jason Junior*, a small remote-controlled robot that could take photographs.

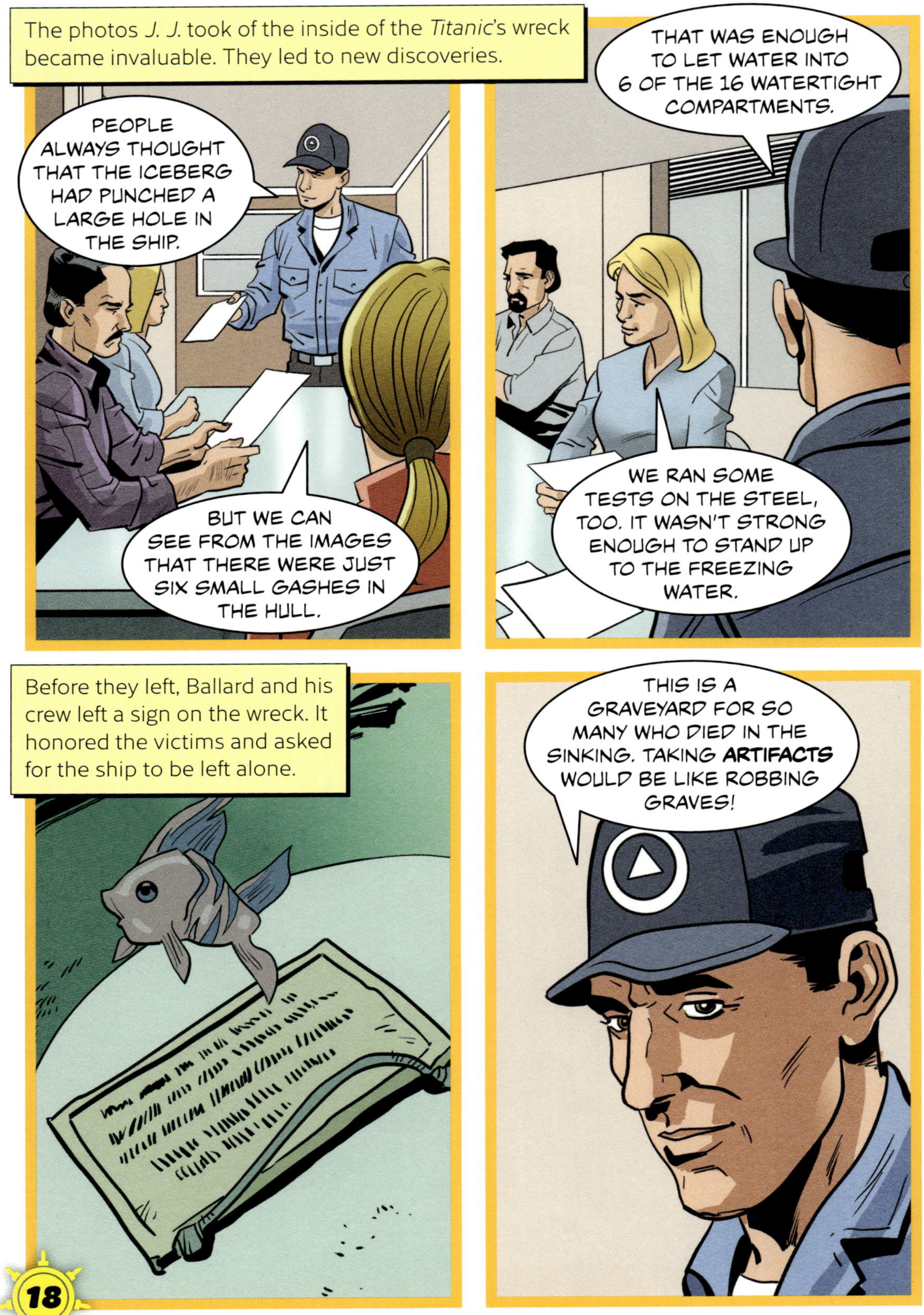
The photos J. J. took of the inside of the Titanic's wreck became invaluable. They led to new discoveries.
PEOPLE ALWAYS THOUGHT THAT THE ICEBERG HAD PUNCHED A LARGE HOLE IN THE SHIP.
BUT WE CAN SEE FROM THE IMAGES THAT THERE WERE JUST SIX SMALL GASHES IN THE HULL.
THAT WAS ENOUGH TO LET WATER INTO 6 OF THE 16 WATERTIGHT COMPARTMENTS.
WE RAN SOME TESTS ON THE STEEL, TOO. IT WASN'T STRONG ENOUGH TO STAND UP TO THE FREEZING WATER.
Before they left, Ballard and his crew left a sign on the wreck. It honored the victims and asked for the ship to be left alone.
THIS IS A GRAVEYARD FOR SO MANY WHO DIED IN THE SINKING. TAKING **ARTIFACTS** WOULD BE LIKE ROBBING GRAVES!

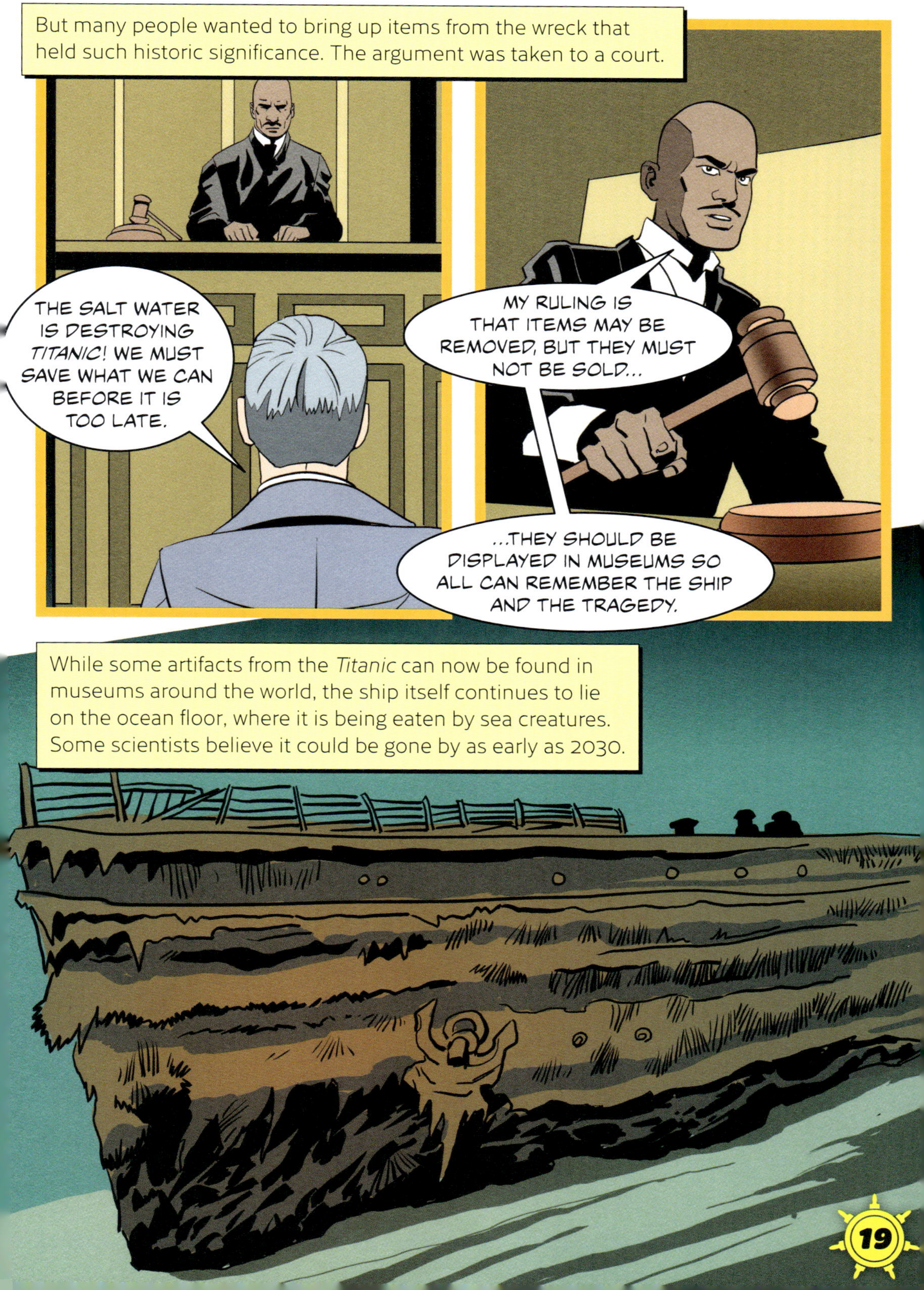
But many people wanted to bring up items from the wreck that held such historic significance. The argument was taken to a court.
THE SALT WATER IS DESTROYING *TITANIC*! WE MUST SAVE WHAT WE CAN BEFORE IT IS TOO LATE.
MY RULING IS THAT ITEMS MAY BE REMOVED, BUT THEY MUST NOT BE SOLD...
...THEY SHOULD BE DISPLAYED IN MUSEUMS SO ALL CAN REMEMBER THE SHIP AND THE TRAGEDY.
While some artifacts from the *Titanic* can now be found in museums around the world, the ship itself continues to lie on the ocean floor, where it is being eaten by sea creatures. Some scientists believe it could be gone by as early as 2030.

Finding a Ship of Dreams

Video cameras and remote-controlled robots helped Ballard and his team explore all corners of the ship. These pictures gave a glimpse into life aboard the ship for its passengers.

Some of the *Titanic*'s artifacts tell us more about the three classes of passengers on board. Dinner plates, for example, came in different styles. There was fine china with a blue and gold design for first-class passengers. In the second class, the less-expensive china was covered with a floral design. There was plain, white china for third-class passengers. Menus found on both victims and survivors show how first-class passengers dined on oysters, lamb, duck, and beef. Meanwhile, third-class passengers were served rice soup and fresh bread, as well as roast beef and boiled potatoes.

A SECOND-CLASS DINNER MENU FROM THE *TITANIC*

TRIPLE SCREW STEAMER "TITANIC."

2ND. CLASS

APRIL 14, 1912.

DINNER.

CONSOMMÉ TAPIOCA

BAKED HADDOCK, SHARP SAUCE

CURRIED CHICKEN & RICE

SPRING LAMB, MINT SAUCE

ROAST TURKEY, CRANBERRY SAUCE

GREEN PEAS PURÉE TURNIPS

BOILED RICE

BOILED & ROAST POTATOES

PLUM PUDDING

WINE JELLY COCOANUT SANDWICH

AMERICAN ICE CREAM

NUTS ASSORTED

FRESH FRUIT

CHEESE BISCUITS

COFFEE

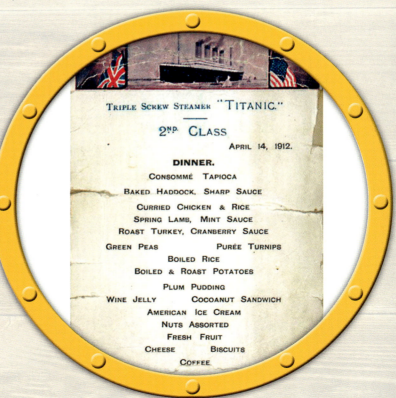

Leather bags on board helped **preserve** some important paperwork, including paperwork for those seeking a new life abroad. One bag held perfume bottles that belonged to a first-class passenger who intended to sell the fragrances in America. **Salvaged** pocket watches even read the time their owners entered the water.

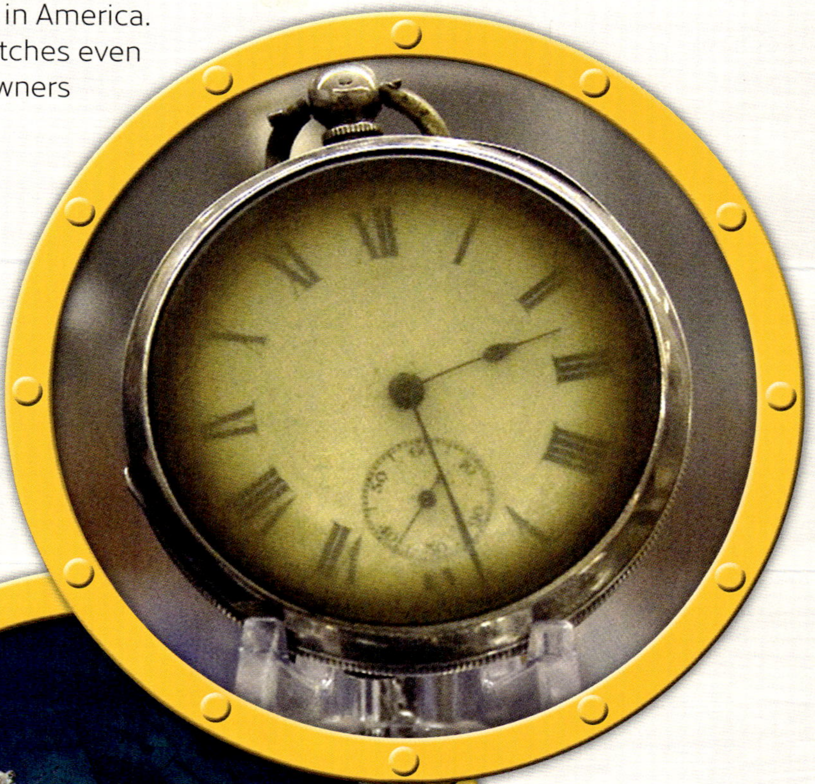

A WATCH FROM AN UNKNOWN PASSENGER, STOPPED AT THE TIME THE *TITANIC* SANK

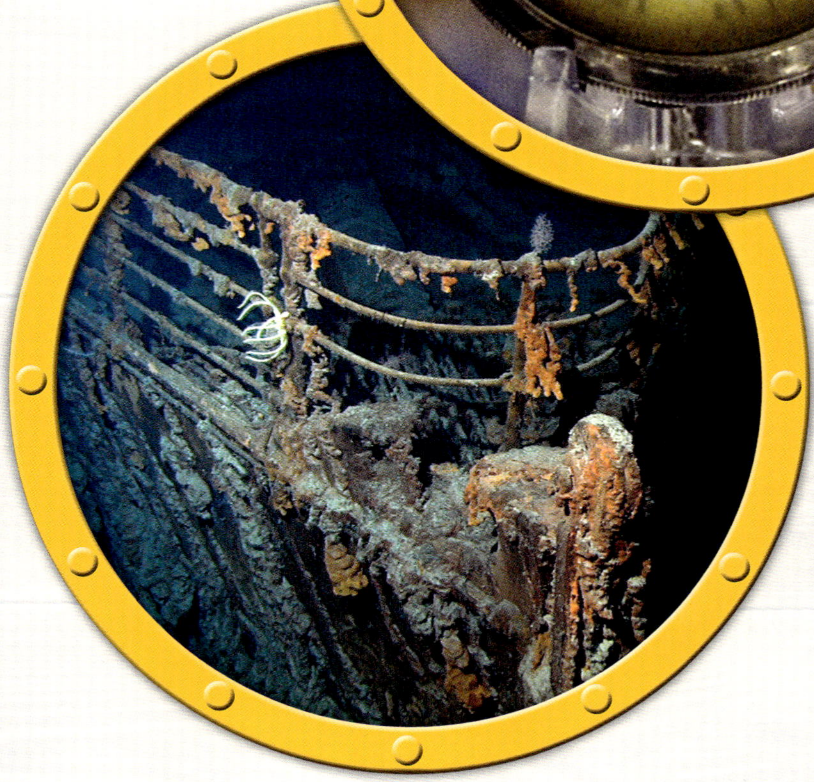

THE BOW OF *TITANIC* AS PHOTOGRAPHED IN JUNE 2004

More Titanic Stories

Robert Ballard has always loved the ocean and has a particular interest in deep-sea exploration. In the 1970s, he helped develop the submersible *Alvin* to explore underwater mountains in the Atlantic Ocean. In 1985, Ballard used his experience and underwater exploratory equipment to be part of the first team to find the sunken ship of dreams. During his career, Ballard discovered many other shipwrecks. He famously requested that *Titanic* be left to honor the dead.

DR. ROBERT BALLARD

EVA HART

Eva Hart was seven when she boarded *Titanic* with her parents. They were traveling across the ocean as second-class passengers to begin a new life in Canada. When the ship struck the iceberg, Eva's father, Benjamin, made sure his wife and daughter safely boarded a lifeboat. They were rescued by RMS *Carpathia*, but Benjamin went down with the sinking ship. Up until her death in 1996, Eva campaigned for *Titanic* to remain a memorial to the dead.

Glossary

artifacts human-made objects

bow the front end of a ship

currents movements of water in an ocean or river

debris field an area that contains the pieces of something that has been destroyed

deck the floor of a ship or boat, especially the upper, open level

elaborate very detailed

hull the main body of a ship, including the bottom, sides, and deck

innovation a new idea or product

luxury expensive and desirable

ocean liner a large, luxurious passenger ship

preserve to protect from harm

salvaged saved from destruction

scavengers animals that feed on dead material

sonar technology that uses sound to find objects under water

stern the back end of a ship

submersible a small underwater vehicle

surface the top layer of something

wreck a sunken ship

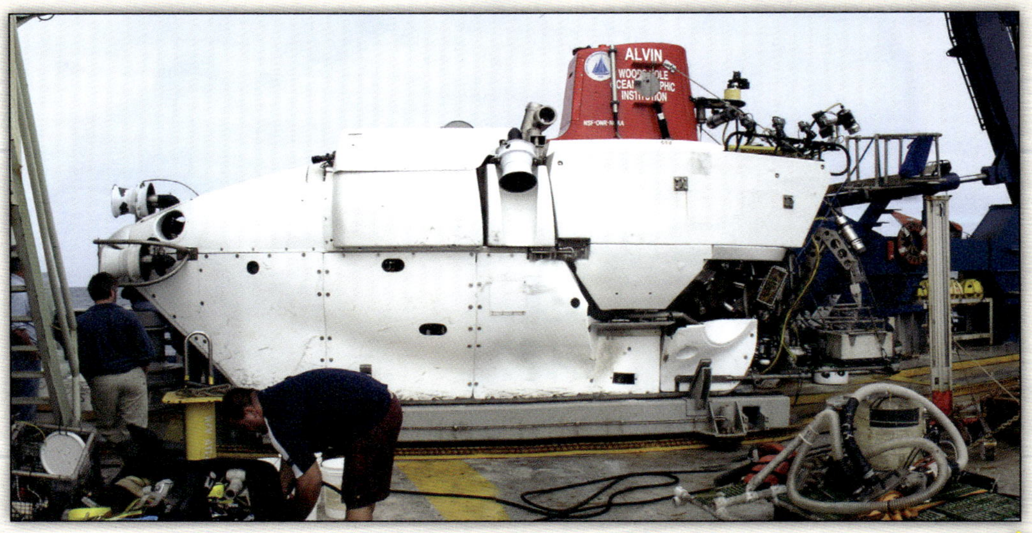
ALVIN

ALVIN THE DEEP-OCEAN RESEARCH SUBMERSIBLE

Index

Alvin 16–17, 22
Argo 11, 13
artifacts 18–20
Ballard, Dr. Robert 9, 11–12, 14, 16–18, 20, 22
Carpathia 8, 22
compartments 18
debris field 9, 11
Hart, Eva 22
iceberg 4, 18, 22
Michel, Jean-Louis 11, 16
museums 19
robot 17, 20
submersible 16, 22
video camera 8, 20
wreckage 7

Read More

Arbuthnott, Gill. *From Shore to Ocean Floor.* Somerville, MA: Candlewick Press, 2023.

Burgan, Michael. *Rediscovering the* Titanic *(A True Book).* New York: Scholastic Inc., 2023.

O'Daly, Anne. *Sunken Ship of Dreams! The* Titanic, *1912 (Doomed History).* Minneapolis: Bearport Publishing Company, 2023.

Learn More Online

1. Go to **FactSurfer.com** or scan the QR code below.
2. Enter "**Discovering Titanic**" into the search box.
3. Click on the cover of this book to see a list of websites.